SO MANY ROOMS

Laura Scott was born in London and now lives in Norwich. Her pamphlet *What I Saw* won the Michael Marks Prize in 2014, and in 2015 she won the Geoffrey Dearmer Prize. Her poems have appeared in various magazines including *PN Review, Oxford Poetry* and *Poetry Review*, and a selection of her work was featured in Carcanet's *New Poetries VII* in 2018.

SO
MANY
ROOMS

LAURA SCOTT

CARCANET

In memory of my mother

First published in Great Britain in 2019 by
Carcanet
Alliance House, 30 Cross Street
Manchester M2 7AQ
www.carcanet.co.uk

A CIP catalogue record for this book is
available from the British Library.
ISBN 978 1 78410 849 6

Book design by Andrew Latimer
Printed in Great Britain by SRP Ltd, Exeter, Devon

The publisher acknowledges financial
assistance from Arts Council England.

CONTENTS

SO MANY ROOMS

IF I COULD WRITE LIKE TOLSTOY

> you'd see a man
dying in a field with a flagstaff still in his hands.

I'd take you close until you saw the grass
blowing around his head, and his eyes

looking up at the white sky. I'd show you
a pale-faced Tsar on a horse under a tree,

breath from its nostrils, creases in gloved fingers
pulling at the reins, perhaps hoof marks in the mud

as he jumps the ditch at the end of the field.
I'd show you men walking down a road,

one of them shouting to the others to get off it.
You'd hear the ice crack as they slipped down the bank

to join him, bringing their horses with them. You'd feel
the blood coming out of the back of someone's head,

warm for a moment, before it touched the snow.
I'd show you a dead man come back to life.

Then I'd make you wait – for pages and pages –
before you saw him, go to his window

and look at how the moon turns half a row
of trees silver, leaves the other half black.

HOW TO LIGHT A CIGARETTE

His voice seems to have just arrived here,
to have come into the room in the loose slack

of a pause when the air had nothing to do
but gather around him as if he were

the hero in a Russian novel, leaning against
the mantelpiece with his hands in his pockets

and the mirror loving him from behind.
Look how he bends his neck, how he cups

his hand as he lights his cigarette before
he answers. Look at her watching the blue grey

smoke unravel into a scurry of notes running
across a stave as she listens to the way

he stresses his consonants, softens his vowels
as he talks of the war in his perfect French.

AND PIERRE?

With his ripe face like one of those pale freckled pears
you hold in your hand and his mind shuddering across it

like a bruise – he's legible to all the world. With his great legs,
broad and strong as the trees, he walks in and out of chapters

smelling of eau de cologne, or an animal that sleeps in a barn.
With his long fingers running across the stubble on his jaw,

he listens to the black Russian rain before he picks up his pen.
With his eyes so blue you'd think he'd drunk the sky down

with all that champagne, he watches the soldiers, (red epaulettes
and high boots) drag that boy to the place where they shoot him.

He watches the boy pull his loose coat tight before he sags and slides
down the post. And when it's all over, he watches them roll him

gently into the hole with the others and before he can look away,
he sees, there in the earth, the boy's shoulder still moving.

TOLSTOY'S DOG

What is it about the lavender grey dog
        hanging around the men
playing with a piece of straw
        as if it were a stick
while Moscow burns behind them?
        What is it that makes her lie
across my mind as if she might be
        what all those words were about?

FRAGMENT

How can I forget the feel of her ribs
under my fingertips,

the thump of her slow heart
into my hand? I will be the frost

running silver threads through brown leaves under her feet –

TO THE TREES

quick and slick
        and full of you,
the you I don't want,
                the you that brims over, brims under my lines, the you I can't
remake, reshape,
                the you I –
        just leave it, drop it, walk away. There's nothing to see here.

Go to the trees,
        I always go to the trees, but let's go
to the tree outside my window,
        the one standing on its own, away from all the others,
the one with the great arms stretching up

the one with too many fingers spreading themselves
        into shapes so the fierce birds might come to them. Too many for what?

To be just pointing at the sky,
        to be just making shapes for the birds?

They must be a trace of something,
        of some hand, some principle urging them on –

maybe Maths or God
        and God knows we don't want to go down that road
                        do we?

Just look at the trees.

I wish I didn't know any rules, any at all, and then my poems,
        or this poem at least,
would move, would soar, would hover and break
        into thousands and thousands
                of pieces of white material.

MULBERRY TREE

My mother made pudding with its fruit,

                     white bread drinking

colour just as the sheets waited

              for the birds to stain them purple.

        A king planted it years ago so his mistress could wear silk.

                  I imagine her dress,

the colour left on the side of your bowl.

ESPALIER

Who was it
      who first thought

of spreading a tree
      across a wall,

of taking its branches
      and fanning them

out like arms
      and legs

across a white sheet?
      How did they know

they'd get bigger, sweeter
      fruit that way?

SOMETHING ABOUT BEING A PLANT
WITHOUT ANY LIGHT

God knows precisely what she said.
I only heard bits of it and the door
was closed. Words came under it

like rats squeezing themselves
flat before they turned and went back
the other way. I pressed my ear

to the door but all I could hear was years
screaming themselves out of the walls,
pleading with her to be lived again.

SO MANY HOUSES

When the grown-ups came we scattered like dust
          into the skirting boards – and watched
as they swirled and whirled and married the wrong people.

So many rooms and so many houses
          they had to spread the paintings
thinly over the walls. We jumped on the beds

and ran in the gardens, climbed all those stairs
          curled our fingers around all those banisters
but we stood still on the landings and felt

the floorboards warp under our feet.
          All those houses but only one pattern
and they made it again and again as if it were a song

they loved and they had to play again and again,
          a song about a girl with skin as white as alabaster
who danced with a man with hair as black as night,

a song about the child he gave her before he left her
          to find another who would give her two more
and as we listened to the song coming through the floorboards

it settled into us and we saw ourselves
          spread out in a deck of cards across the table,
a fan of children with different coloured hair.

AND THOSE WALLS CAME INTO OUR GAME

My mother took us to my godmother's flat with silver

    swords hanging on walls and silhouettes

of boys in uniforms – all high-ceilinged Regency drawing room

    at the front

        damp maid's kitchen and bathroom at the back,

shabby like a Fortuny dress

    that has lost its pleats.

A flat in a town where houses were carved

    into flats and streets –

cut crescents of beige stone.

She let us go to the park on our own until we'd learned

    the shape of its banks and how to lean

        over the bridge and wait like children in a book

for the sounds of trains bursting into the light.

She told us he'd be gone when we got back

and her words

were bubbles in my drink, swimming up to my mouth.

AND THE SEA GOT INTO YOUR HAIR

To have sugar like sand around your feet
to feel the fear prickling up your calves
to hear him shouting and find yourself

thrown out of your own throat while they
stand and watch – his face still angry, hers
harder to read, turning away from you.

To be that child, with the garden behind you.
To sit on those trees nobody ever cut
and dip your feet in and out of the grass

while the branch moves up and down
like a horse under your weight.
To be that girl inside the white square

of the photograph, eyes squinting
in the sun, hair wet from the sea
slicked into dark spikes around your neck.

Almost a bounce before it shudders and fans
its blue and white into a new pattern
around my feet. Pieces of china, sharp
as mountain tops cutting through cloud,
tempt me to bend down and trace their shape
with my finger, to feel their lines run
into the chalky grey grain that was always
lurking under the glaze.

                   Next the milk bottles:
two in each hand, cool and wet with drops of dew
still clinging to their fat necks, slippery
between my fingers. I brush one, lightly,
against the arm of a chair – that's all it needs
to make it cry out and they fall like pears
from a tree, hitting the ground and turning it
into a lake of cream and glass, freezing me
to the spot.

              And then the chandelier I used to look at
with my opera glasses held the wrong way around,
so all those festoons of crystal beads became something
you might find in a rich girl's doll's house.
I imagined how the weight of it would rip the plaster
from the ceiling before it crashed onto the heads
of the people in the red stalls below; the tinkling
of the glass droplets falling through the air
more beautiful than anything the orchestra ever found
in their pit.

            Big break last: my grandmother's bowls
stacked at the back of the cupboard, their glass worn
soft and grey – all my mother had left. She cried
when I broke one and even then, I understood why.

BUSTER KEATON

Find a stone that reminds you of the moon.
Hold it in your hand until it becomes a face
smooth and cold in your palm.

Blink away the colour from your eyes
and you might see him flickering
in black and white, moving across the film

of your eye like bits of branch blown
across a dusty road. Look at him
adjusting his hat, finding the balance.

Blameless eyes looking straight at you
as the house collapses around him,
blessing him with its open window.

Maybe they're like fish
swimming inside you,
waiting for someone
to tap the glass.

SOMEWHERE

I've always loved the bit when they're through
the gates but they haven't seen the Wizard yet,
when they're whisked off to be buffed and brushed.

The tin man is oiled and polished, the scarecrow
rolled and restuffed, like a plump cigarette,
the lion sits on a chair while they curl his mane

and file his claws, Dorothy has her hair brushed
and a red bow, even Toto gets clipped. I loved that
place, a pearl hanging on a necklace somewhere

between Oz and Kansas, where the flying monkeys
can't get us and our voices aren't breaking yet
with that cry of home rushing up our throats.

THE LESSON

Unity Spencer, the daughter of Stanley Spencer and Hilda Carline, remembers her mother giving her her first oil painting lesson on Hampstead Heath.

That day still and white

       as a layer of sand caught

in a small glass dome, that day bright like a painting hung at the end

       of a dark hallway.

And then the wind that came from nowhere – so sharp

       she tied her scarf in a soft knot around my neck

before she told me how green

       hides in yellow, waiting for you in the shadows

if you know how to look.   I didn't believe her so she bent down

       and picked a buttercup, pulled it up, out of the grass and held it

between her thumb and forefinger and I remember how I loved the long O

       of her fingers – like an eye. I can still see it now.

But then she opened up her coat and drew back one side of it in a great

       black wing and held the flower against it

and I saw   the green that was always there

        holding the yellow   up and out

so it spun in front of our eyes.

      And her watching me and that voice, the drawl and the break in it

as she said my name – 'Darling Unity', draping it over me

        like lights on a Christmas tree.

TURNER

His father saw it before anyone else,
the boy could paint light, could take the sky
into the bristles of his brush and lay it flat
like ribbon around a haberdasher's card.

He could take the curl of cloud, the line
of sea, and drop them on to canvas
pinned and waiting for him like a spider's
web on a window pane. He could make

colours his father had never seen appear
in white china bowls, grinding red lead
and smalt, madder and green slate
while his father washed bundles of hair

ready for the next day, rolling them
between finger and thumb, smoothing
the shafts flat as fish scales. In the morning,
when the light was at its sharpest, Joseph lit

the colour with water and gum, stirring in
honey so the Prussian blues and milky greens,
the scarlets and viridians, could breathe across
the hatched threads of the canvas. And while

his father knotted and threaded the hair
into silken caps, weaving it into clusters
of curls, the boy split shafts of light
until they shimmered on the tip of his brush.

And for a moment, the father looked up
from his work and was scared by the boy
who could paint God's light across the water,
the air's joy at being empty handed.

DIRECTION

I want to move
       like the blackbird
I saw hopping on the grass
       head cocked
to the side as if it were
       absent-mindedly
going the wrong way
       before it turned
on a wing and flew off
       in the other direction.

COVE

I want to be in that place
        where the myths are still

soft as they leave your lips,
        where I can see the heroes

start to move with their names
        like jewels, hanging

around their necks.
        I want to be there

where their strides are so strong
        all I can do is follow them,

where, if I look into the distance,
        I can see Helen's mother

plaiting her hair and washing
        the clothes in those pools

scooped out of rocks.
        I want to be where the wars

haven't started but the weapons
        are glinting in the sun.

I want to see the tendons
        in a raised heel and the veins

in a horse's flank, I want to be
        in that inlet where,

if I stop listening to you, for a moment
        I can feel the wake

of a boat slapping against
        the helm of my mind.

HOW TO CATCH A GOD

the river god Ilissos, from the west pediment of the Parthenon

It's all about desire, you have to get that, you have to find a way
        to push it into the stone – make it big

because there's so much of it and it keeps moving and flowing
        like the river. There's his, to pull himself

out of the water onto the land, there's ours, to watch him, to see him
        in the act of making a new gorgeous line of himself,

and there's yours, to show us, to draw the desire from its source,
        to spin it and circle it, so its truth ripples

through the marble and we feel it in the slant of him, as we circle him
        and see his breath move like water

through his lungs, and the space between his thighs and the cracked scar
        that cuts across the back of him and imagine,

for a moment, that it's us – no, not us, me – he is turning towards,
        my body that will feel the weight of his.

That's what you have to do to beckon him down from the mountain
        and push the warmth and the ease of him

into your cold stone. Start with that notch at the base of his throat,
        carve that thimble where the bone coves.

And then follow and hollow out the line that runs from there as it
        meanders and trickles through his pectorals

and under the swerve of his ribs. Open up the space between rib and hip
   until we hear them call out to each other

across the smooth stone of his skin. Slow time with your hands so its
   pendulum hangs heavy and suspended in that moment

before movement, when the muscles are still and soft, waiting to harden
   and contract. Make his torso lean on a hand

that's no longer there. Splay its rays so we think we see him press
   down on its palm to catch the mass of himself

and haul it up like a magnificent fish pulled dripping and gleaming
   out of the river. And when you've done that, you're nearly there.

All you need to do now is seal out death, it has no place here.
   It casts no shadow on this stone.

SISTERS

I bring them into the house on a white day when the sea
has taken all the blue back to the waves and lie them
on their sides while I find the red vase with the pattern
of trees and bridges running around its base.
And then the yellow one slows me, shows me its petals
like parchment, so many crinkled together a foxglove
could creep in unnoticed and hide amongst them.
How did you get here, old rose, were you smuggled
through a chink in the years on to the walls of my garden?
Or dropped out of a window in a dark-panelled room
up above the river? You should be sung about or woven
into a conceit of thorns. You share the vase, here
on my desk with your younger sisters who hold their shape
and release their scent more prudently than you ever will.

THE BANKER'S DAUGHTER
ALLAN RAMSAY 1759

As soon as he saw her he knew – he'd do her as
a half-length with a three quarters view of the head,
maybe a greeny grey behind her – that was how to coax

her face out of the doorway and into the room of his stare.
He liked the cut of her, the blunt edge of her jaw,
the cool way she looked back at him.

He'd get her to sit at one end of the sofa and watch her
arrange herself amongst her skirts and sleeves,
gathering her potential into the creases of her clothes

like a swan folding its wings back into their tips
as it settles on to the water. He'd wait for her to look up,
unguarded for a moment, so he got a flicker of the face

he wanted to paint before she pulled it back into the space
behind the eyes only practised sitters find. Later, when it
started to blur, he'd swill the image of her around in his head

like brandy warming in a glass. For now, he'd start with lines
– the slope of the sofa behind her to balance the tilt of her head,
the angle of her arms, down and out to the elbows,

back to the centre to meet on her lap. And finally the lines
of the black lace shawl framing the pleats of her bodice.
He'd paint the lace opening out into its pattern of loss

across her shoulder, the cinnabar pink of her dress behind it,
the froth of her cuffs, the soft folds of peach silk around
her throat. Only then would he start on the face,

building up layers of lead white to get the smoothness
of her forehead running back into the dark arc of her hair.
And as he waited for the thick paint to dry, he'd look

at what he'd done, pulsing as it set on to the canvas
and he'd find himself thinking of the goose egg he held as a boy,
the shudder in his fingers as they stretched around its shape,

the jolt in his stomach when he held it up to the candle
and he saw the blood vessels moving in the light,
and the heart beating right up against the shell.

DAUGHTER

A girl plays in the long grass under the tree
her hair cutting the air like a horse's tail

darting in and out of imagined rooms
finding paths through blades of green.

*

Skin white as rice cooked with lemon
left to cool on a blue plate in the sun

soft like suede under my hand
pulls me to her like a horse to water.

*

Her voice is thrown all over the house,
as if she were scattering seed into the earth

of every room as she runs past, or leaving
threads of herself to slow me as I walk by.

*

When you go away she sleeps in our bed,
fizzing like sherbert, waiting for me

to come back to her, unrecognisable,
her face still in sleep's hand.

*

In the last fold of the night, before the day
ruffles its feathers, I see her falling down the stairs

in someone else's house, the small of her back
hitting their cruel steps again and again.

*

Only dark red leaves left on the trees
the same colour as her hair

running down the back of her black coat
ahead of me this morning.

*

I watch her on a loop as she cartwheels
across the room with new precision

the softness lopped from her limbs as she goes,
a swoop of grief takes me in its arms.

*

I am like damp sand collapsing into itself
trying to remember the heel of a girl

now swimming in the sea. All I can do
is make lines for her to shimmer in.

THE FALLING

all those girls
their paper knees
folding under them

and the tree so still
and the wind running
fingers through the leaves

all those girls
their long smooth hair
waiting, waiting for someone

anyone to run their fingers
through it
and the tree so still

pulling them under it
back to it
to carve their initials

into its hard soft skin
all those girls crumpling
falling like song birds

out of the sky
and a mother
a poor mother

out in the night
dragging her daughter
pulling her out of the water

holding her up
waiting, waiting
for the breath to come

COWS

They bothered us like flies, those great cows with heads
as big as dogs and flanks like tanks twitching in the sun.
They spent their days churning up the paths that ran
in broken lines through the folds of our map. We didn't listen

to stories of walkers trampled to death, breathing their last
under those weirdly delicate legs, or tales of strange new breeds
rampaging through the fields like giant hogweed.
We gave them a wide berth, hugging the field's edge instead

and left the cows to loll in the middle. We climbed a hill
and sat with our backs against a wall when a whole gang of bullocks
appeared, snorting and staring at us with their glossy eyes.
We scrambled over the wall, flinging children, dogs, sandwiches

into the air. And then they wandered off – all except one
– who stood looking at my daughter, as if his huge cow heart
was beating just for her. Those in the sea of fields around our house
were different, like cows on a tin of Caran D'Ache pencils.

One evening we got back to find one lying on her side
with her head held up so she could look at her new black son,
still wet but already trying out his new legs. We missed the bit
when she got to her feet, but when we looked again,

there she was licking him dry, his frame buckling a little
under the weight of her tongue. My daughter loved that –
the way he leant into her, the way the bulk of her steadied him.
That night, a sound came from the cow's throat and folded itself

into the creases of my dream, and I saw her, falling back
into the grass, leaving the calf standing where she had been.
In the morning I went to the window and there she was,
lying in the field like something washed up by the tide.

And that image hung itself, unsteadily, in my head,
rocking slowly between death and sleep. Once my daughter
had seen her, and turned her face back to mine, I knew.
I tried to undo the knot that had held them together, telling her

the herd would look after him. As the light left the sky something
pulled him back to her, made him chase the gathering crows
away before he folded up his legs and settled himself next to her.
In the morning, she was gone and my daughter's face had changed.

WAITING FOR MY LIFE TO BEGIN

I saw them skim the fence of your teeth
and slide out into the room. And I envied you,

oh how I envied you with all the four chambers of my heart –
to be bored like that, bored like an aristocrat

lying on a sofa somewhere in a room where the windows
stretch all the way down to the floor and the walls are blue

as the eyes of peacock feathers. *Waiting for my life to begin*
that's what you said, under your breath maybe

but you said it, in those words, those very words.

PIGEON

The soft thud of it
          as it hit the car,

feathers floating
          up like smoke

rising into the blue
          on a packet of gitanes.

I've always thought
          too much of death,

let it hang around
          my ankles like a child

you drag across the floor.
          I never found

the right broom
          to shoo it away.

FENCE

What is it about the fence that scares me? you know the one
I mean, the one with gaps between its narrow wooden slats
and a length of wire running across its back. Is it the way
it leans and sags into the grass that grows on the dunes?
Or maybe the way it creaks as it sways in the wind, the way it moves
like seaweed breathing in the tide. Is it because it can't keep anything
in or anything out? Or is it because, despite all that, it's found
the strength in the slant, the speck of stillness that hides
itself somewhere on the point of collapse? I think I know –
but I wish I didn't, so I'll make the turn as fast as I can, so fast
you'll only just see me do it. It reminds me of you
in that white room, taking too long to die, stopping
and starting, huffing and puffing your way to the door,
dragging your great ribs into the leaves like an old bear.

THE HALF-LOVED

Sometimes you hear her, breathing heavily,
climbing the stairs to find you in the room
where the old silk wallpaper still clings
to the walls. And then you feel her sighs

tightening around your ribs as she rehearses
her lines one more time so she can tell you
exactly where you went wrong in a voice that cuts
through your chest. Sometimes you see her

swaying in the doorway, churning the ground
under her feet like Hannibal's last elephant,
tired of all that armour cutting into the folds of her skin.
Sometimes you taste her in the dregs of your wine,

swirling in the bottom of your glass and then,
she cuts you off, mid-swallow, until your throat
remembers all those conversations you turned
with a skier's grace when they got to the precipice

where the love should have been. The half-loved
remembers everything – every slight you ever dealt her,
every letter you sent her. Sometimes she runs
her fingers over the white space around your name

until the paper is as soft as cloth, and pictures you
putting down your pen and thinking of someone
else. The half-loved saw it all, blinked it in
through her dark lashes, and is weeping it out today.

THE THORN AND THE GRASS

That day I ran my fingers over my son's knee
and they slowed as if puzzled by a sudden patch
of hardness where the skin thickened and pulled
me back to trace the contour lines around it. And there
in the middle of his soft flesh that black pin prick
puncturing his creamy skin and my fingers pressing
down on the ridge around it and us watching as a tip slowly
emerged, pushing its nose up into the air. So I pressed
a little harder and this great thorn slid out of his knee,
the unmistakable curve of a rose thorn freed from his flesh.
But then what about the grass, shall I make her the grass
that grows in the cold sand high above the beach,
blown sad and sharp by the wind, swishing her blades
from side to side, waiting for him to run through her?

A DIFFERENT TUNE

oh my heavy heart how can I
make you light again so I don't have to

lug you through the years and rooms?
Shall I make a sling for you of silk and fingers

in a blue that brings out your bruised red?
I could hang it from the bony strut

of my collarbones to hammock your sad weight.
Would you soften your walls and open

your dark chambers if I did? I'm the one –
the only one – who really loves you

so be light for me, light like the bird
perching on the rose stem, its pronged feet

threaded through the black thorns –
so light the stem barely moves.

THE SINGING

I heard it in that weirdly wintery room where the velvet curtains
fell in liver-coloured scrolls and crept out from the walls
when they found the floor and the dark wood cabinet waited
in the corner. That was where they sang for us, or for each other,

or for Greece. I'm not sure who – all I know is the sound of it,
its swell and its swoon, the swerve of it as it left their fingers
and throats and pulled the air into new shapes around us.
And if I circle it, slowly, with these lines, go round the outside of it,

some of that sound might slide into your ears. If I told you
what they looked like, the three musicians, the fat one
in the middle with his bald head and his great belly
arranged over his thighs, more like a butcher than a musician,

and the other two sitting impassively on either side, as if they were bored
– then maybe you'd see them sitting there, with the windows
and the velvet curtains behind them. You'd see me in the front row,
shifting in my seat, wondering when they were going to start.

And then you'd watch the bald one thread his hand under the neck
of his guitar and lay the other over its body and start to play
and the sounds of those notes, higher and faster than you'd expect
would fall into the room like leaves as he moves his fingers

quickly over the fret board. And that would be enough, easily enough,
you could sit and listen to the sharp sounds of the strings
climbing the air forever, but then he'd give you his voice as well
and you won't be able to believe that such a voice could come

from such a source. And some bit of you would back away like a horse
rearing up on its hind legs, troubled by something its rider can't see
because you won't know where to put the sound, what to do with it.
And you'll wonder why the other two are there, they're not doing anything,

just looking at the floor but they don't look bored anymore.
But then the old one with the slicked-back hair will start to hum, and the sound
will be as deep and dark as the lines on his face. And when the song starts
its ascent, the other man will come in and the three voices will plait

themselves together until the tune is so strong you could climb up it.
And the air will be so taut, you'll hear the breath caught
in the back of your own throat. And then the song will swerve downwards
in its layered refrain and the audience around and behind you

add their voices to the musicians' and all the voices will go down together
as if the song had stairs and they were made of stone
and the voices were like the soles of thousands of shoes lapping away
at the stone year after year until there is a dent in the middle of the step.

And you'll follow them, wishing you knew the words, willing the song
to go on pouring itself into the room. And that layer that locks you
into yourself will fall away and you'll remember Caliban, crying out
when he wakes from his dream and longs to hear that song again.

Rumours buzz around them like flies. Some say
they've taken over the old airport in Athens,
roaming its runways, loping around
the abandoned planes, cocking their legs on the clumps
of grass growing through the cracks in the tarmac.
Somebody has actually seen them, sleeping
on the unmoving baggage carousels and chewing
the dead cables, howling under the announcement boards
proclaiming flight details of planes long gone.
There are stories of them guarding the Acropolis at night
in return for scraps of food, of thousands of them
being rounded up and driven away in lorries
before the Olympics, and poisoned or released into the hills,
depending on who you're talking to. They say the ones
in the towns are fine, they spend their days lying in the shade
and their nights strolling around the bars and restaurants.
But the ones at the edges where the roads turn into motorways
and the grass grows tall and thick, they're the ones you have to watch.
They have started to pack and someone has drawn black lines
around their pale lemon eyes. The bitches are always on heat
and the litters are getting bigger. The pups with the soft pink
paw pads are the first to go and soon their own mothers
will be breaking their necks before they've opened their eyes.
And one day a man will come home, dressed as a beggar,
a man who has been travelling for years and years but this time
there will be no dog flattening its ears and thumping its tail
at the sight of him, this time there'll be wolves
circling the scrubland where he swears his house used to be.

THE PHOTOGRAPH OF TWO GIRLS

May 2014, Uttar Pradesh

They hung them high up. Girl cousins split between
the branches of a great mango tree. One in red,
the other in green – colours so bold for a moment,
you blink and in that dark sweep of lid across eye

you pretend someone has draped the tree in swathes of cloth
and that's all you're looking at – blocks of colours running
in strange waterfalls down to the ground. But then you see
the feet and the hair, oiled and plaited and the way their necks

slump like broken stems in their scarves, and the bodies sway
back into the frame. You notice the girl in green is higher
than the girl in red, so high her feet are clear and sharp in the air,
while her cousin's blur in the dust just above the ground.

And then your eyes move out from the branches
to take in the crowd gathered around the base of the tree,
women sitting in a circle, men and boys standing awkwardly
amongst them. A net of villagers thrown around the girls,

like a thicket of thorns grown too late to keep them safe
but enough to slow the men who come in their uniforms
to cut them down – some of them the same men who
found the girls the night before in the fields, who held them

down and split them open, who shared them out as if they were
fruit to be scraped out of their skins. And so they stay a little longer,
to be seen by all the world, those untouchable girls
in their bold colours, hanging in the branches of a mango tree.

CAN'T STAND THEM

               loathe them, always have, ever since
I was a child. Probably something to do with the wretched

nightingale in that story they used to read to me, piercing
its heart on a thorn and singing the white rose red before

it dies and its little corpse falls to the ground. The fleshy ones
are the worst, sucking up all the rain and all that cellulose,

or whatever its called, swelling inside them and the way
I can't stop myself cutting into them with my nail to leave

a crescent-shaped mark on their stems. And then the smell
they leave in the water in the bottom of the vase, the way

it curls into my nostrils. Lilies are so obvious, so banal,
but the hydrangeas with their heads as big as cabbages,

obsequiously bowing to me, like supplicants every time
I walk past. I like it when the rain bruises their tiny petals.

WHAT I KNOW

is this   this

is what I *really* know, this is what tocks

and ticks inside me, this is what seeps out –

my signature scent, the one that catches

in the fine hairs of your nostrils so you can sniff me out in a room full of people.

This is what paper-cuts my throat and clouds the trees

that grow in the soft bed of my lungs.

This is what I know and what I know is this –

you've watched me and clocked me and found me

wanting.   That's where I am

caught here in this smear with you

running your cold carp eyes over my words and recognising their lack,

my lack, my heaving lack, the one I carry on my back –

that's what I know   that's what I write

while others tweet and fleet in a silver shoal up to the light.

IF I WERE A FISH

I'd swim into your head
as, waiting for sleep, you lay on your side. I'd dart from temple

to temple until you felt the curve of my silver belly skim
the muddy sheets of your brain. I'd stir up your silt

with a flick of my tail and your lips would be as cold
as mine as we chased the river's mouth back to the sea.

And you'd watch as they hauled me up in their nets, see me
swallow fistfuls of air before they laid me on a marble slab

and the cold stilled my gills. You'd turn away as their knife
slit me open like a letter. And when they dropped me

into the yellow froth of butter, I'd cry out as my flesh
hissed in the heat of the pan, my translucence evaporating –

but you wouldn't hear. You'd sip your wine
with your fork still in your hand,

tell them I tasted of mud.

BOX

Open it, push back its hinged lid. It's easy, so much easier
than you thought. All you have to do is line up its sides

with your middle fingers then lift it, lightly. You'll hear
the wood unsettle itself around the joint and you might see

its knots and whirls loosen and unwind into the grain. Look inside –
and there he is turning towards you, because you're in there too,

you're about to put your hand on the side of his face and when you do,
he'll kiss you. And life is arching its back to where it should be,

where it wants to be – but that's only half of it. Stay with this.
Don't pick up your phone to scroll through all the messages

and read them to the end. Stay with what it felt like to have him,
balance that on the apex of an arch somewhere inside you,

to have him, and how afterwards he sat next to you in the back
of someone else's car, the line of him, the side of him, right up against you.

SOMETIMES WHEN I CAN'T SLEEP

I see myself   caught in a clot of time – younger

on the back of someone's motorbike with my arms bent

            and held in an L shape

        carefully around him and my face right up against his back, so close

I could have laid my cheek on the leather of his jacket and he's a friend's older brother

            taking me all the way   from Brixton

to Hammersmith   then back again and we're threading

        through the Friday night air and the streets and cars, swerving

and zig-zagging.   And we stop at a red light

and he turns around to look at me, and he pushes up his visor

        to tell me I'm a good passenger

            and I love him

just for that second and we're off again and I'm leaning

        into the bends.

SEWING

Sew until the light has left the sky.
Sew until your arm has found its grace
up and to the side, up and to the side.

Sew until the nape of your neck softens
as you turn to look at the leaves falling
on the other side of the glass.

Look at them falling into the night.
Someone has been here before you
with a thread thicker and blacker than yours,

squeezing it flat between finger and thumb.
Sew until you see the folds of her years
pulled into place by your stitch.

THE GREY MIRROR

'I want a poem I can grow old in'
EAVAN BOLAND

Maybe it was there all the time, in the room with the high ceiling
and the fireplace and the mirror rimmed in gold above it,

and if I went back to that house in Ireland where she took us in
out of the rain, I'd find it. If I stood in front of the mirror I'd see

how grey and speckled with black its glass was and then I'd see
lines spreading around my eyes like rays in a child's drawing

of the sun. And if someone called my name from somewhere else,
in another part of the house, I'd turn my head to answer them,

and the ligaments in my neck would push against my skin
and I'd catch sight of their slanting lines in the mirror.

And my voice would sound different – older, softer, sadder
maybe, like the fine rain that blows and falls outside the house.

There'd be a lag in it, a space where one sound stretched
out to reach the next. And in the slack of that lag the words would

start to feel they could go anywhere – out of the window and up to the sky
above the sea to watch the mountains forming and collapsing

on the top of the waves, and then, fast as a whippet, they'd turn
and rush back to the shore at low tide to pluck a green-lipped mussel

off its rope. And I watch them as they pushed into its black hinge to prise it open and draped themselves over the frills of its flesh.

And I'd let them because now I'm old I know, they always go back to the sea.

IN WHICH SHE LEARNS THE LOST CHILDREN
ARE NEVER FOUND, ONLY REMEMBERED

It starts, it always starts, with her
watching them and everything else blurring around them

as they burst through the water's skin (again and again)
the years running off their limbs

the water washing them
back to what they were when she could still balance the weight

of each of them in turn on her left hip. That's how it starts.
The next move is when she tries to blink the sight of them

on to the back of her mind's eye so she can pull them out like a photo
from a drawer

but her eyes water and cloud –
so she tries something else:

to throw words around them like towels,
to pause the great gush of life of them into an aria

she can sing (again and again)

but the sun is so hot and anyway they're doing something else now.
It's nearly over when she gives up, she forgets

everything and her eyes clear.

But then the swallows come clipping and dipping the pool
 with their wings and beaks.

Try again say the swallows
but what do they know of time?

OUR LADY OF AUGUST

High above the town
on the apex
of a golden triangle

she spreads
her black wings
into grey sky.

Clouds move
like bad dreams
around her.

Her body a trunk of stone.
The sound of men
singing to each other,

bragging so beautifully
with the rain running
down their necks.

If the wings could cut loose
they'd pull her up
and up into the heavens

above the palazzos
and circling squares,
up to where the horses go

in their heads as they
sweat and foam
around the sanded square.

The first time I heard it, its notes went through me
like milk through water, clouding into my bones
so I knew the end before it had even begun.

I sat and listened as you told me the story of the old man
and his three daughters, how he loved them all
but only one of them was good – the one who asked

for a rose instead of a dress, who talked of salt
instead of gold, who stood still and said nothing
while her sisters ran up and down flights of words.

And as the story drew itself around me, I saw her
sitting at a table, dragging her nail across the yolk,
rucking its film up into creases until it split

and the yellow pumped out into the white: that's when
it all went wrong, the beast threw back his head
and roared until the leaves shook on the trees,

the meat wouldn't cure, and the fish started to rot
as soon as they left the sea, the kingdom split
into a thousand pieces and blew back into the old man's eyes

like sand. And I waited for you to tell me about the mother –
how she loved this daughter best of all, stroking her hair
when she carried her back to the house at the end of the day.

ACKNOWLEDGEMENTS

Thanks to the editors of the following publications in which some of these poems have appeared: *Poetry Review*, *Oxford Poetry*, *The Rialto*, *Magma*, *PN Review*, *New Poetries 7*, *The Scores*, *The Compass* and *Tate ETC*.

'How to catch a god' was commissioned by the Poetry Society and the British Museum for the Rodin and the art of ancient Greece exhibition 2018.